Words
for Lent

Edited by Nicola Slee

International Bible Reading Association

This book contains material previously published in *Words for Today 2010*.

The International Bible Reading Association's scheme of readings is listed monthly on the Christian Education website at www.christianeducation.org.uk/ibra_scheme.php and the full scheme may be downloaded in English, Spanish and French.

Cover photograph: Steve Trevett
Editor: Nicola Slee

Published by:
The International Bible Reading Association
1020 Bristol Road
Selly Oak
Birmingham B29 6LB
United Kingdom

Charity number 211542

ISBN 978-1-905893-40-9

Designed and typeset by GCS, Leighton Buzzard, Beds.
Printed and bound by Simlex Group Limited, Enterprise Drive, Four Ashes, Wolverhampton WV10 7DF

Acknowledgements and abbreviations

GNB   Good News Bible (The Bible Societies/Collins Publishers) – Old Testament © American Bible Society 1976; New Testament © American Bible Society 1966, 1971, 1976.

NIV   Scripture quotations taken from The Holy Bible, New International Version © 1973, 1978, 1984 by International Bible Society. Used by permission of Hodder & Stoughton Limited. All rights reserved. 'NIV' is a registered trademark of International Bible Society. UK trademark number 1448790.

NJB   Taken from the New Jerusalem Bible, published and copyright 1985 by Darton, Longman and Todd Ltd and Doubleday & Co. Inc., and used by permission of the publishers.

NSRV   New Revised Standard Version © 1989, Division of Christian Education of the National Council of Churches of Christ in the United States of America.

REB   Revised English Bible© Oxford University and Cambridge University Presses 1989.

RSV   The Holy Bible, Revised Standard Version © 1973, Division of Christian Education of the National Council of Churches of Christ in the United States of America.

BCE   Before the Common Era. BCE and CE are used by some writers instead of BC and AD.

Contents

Wednesday 6th March
~~Thurs~~ 18th April.

Prayers

O God, make me real
and ready to hear you speaking in the lives
of the people I shall meet today and the places I shall go to or hear about.

Nicola Slee

Lord, help us to let go of whatever hinders us
from seeing things from your perspective
and help us to recognize the signs
that show your kingdom
is even now actively at work in our midst.

Edmund Banyard

Lord God,
we believe that your revelation comes to every nation
in its real and concrete situation;
Help us to see you more clearly in our tradition and culture.
Lord God, we believe that you have called us
to be your hands and feet in this land.
Help us to be living witnesses
of your love and grace to all people . . .
May your justice and peace reign among us.

Charles Klagbo, Togo

May God give us new visions,
to take advantage of new possibilities,
to go out and reach new people.
May the Holy Spirit empower us to do this work.

Josef Ceruenak, Czechoslovakia

You are the Way we shall walk.
You are the Truth we shall take into ourselves.
You are the Life we shall enjoy for ever
and share with all.

Donald Hilton

Introduction

Lent has always been a time of solemn preparation in the church, as disciples seek to enter into the way of the cross and share, insofar as we can, the struggles of Jesus as he faces towards Jerusalem. In the early church, Lent was the main time in the year when new believers, or catechumates, were prepared for baptism and full membership, culminating in a long vigil on Easter Eve and their initiation into the Body of Christ in the first eucharist of Easter Day. Nowadays, Lent is one of the main times when many churches and individual Christians try to take seriously the call to study, pray, fast and commit themselves to the challenge of God's kingdom in some special, or more focused, way. Many folks join Lent groups, give up some luxury or commit themselves to acts of solidarity and social justice. Some churches have recovered the ancient tradition of using Lent as a time for preparing new believers. So there is a sense of Lent being a significant season both for those new to faith, just beginning their journey of discipleship, and those who have been walking in the way of Christ for many years. All of us are called to this journey of deepening commitment, wherever we are on the journey and whoever we are.

We hope that this resource, written by a range of *Words for Today* writers, will be of value to both individuals and groups during Lent, whether you are very new to faith, or whether you have walked this season many, many times before. Our writers are drawn from different parts of the world, different denominations, different theological and spiritual traditions, and different perspectives on the Bible. We hope that each, in their unique way, will cast fresh light on Luke's text, and help readers to walk afresh the road towards the cross and beyond, to Easter joy and resurrection.

Nicola Slee

Editor

Beginnings

1 Theme introduction

Preparing for the week

In this week's readings from Luke's gospel, we consider the work of John the Baptist in preparing the way for Jesus, we recall Jesus' baptism and temptations in the wilderness, and the beginning of his teaching and healing ministry in Nazareth.

In his mission statement in the sermon in the synagogue at Nazareth (Luke 4:16-27), Jesus becomes the herald and agent of liberation to the poor, the one who puts the content of their hope into words and then devotes his life to its fruition. We are called to share in this mission – requiring us to become 'poor in spirit', willing to let go of worldly power and status and identify ourselves with those who are marginalised and commit ourselves to their liberation. Poverty is not good in itself, but where it leads to a deeper dependence on God and coexists with generosity it can be a rare grace – remember Jesus marvelling at the widow's mite (Mark 12:41-44). This week, we are invited to consider both the poverty that must be resisted and that which must be embraced.

For further thought and prayer

- Does insecurity make me more self-seeking and less caring about the needs of others, lessening my humanity, clouding my sense that people matter more than money?
- Or does our current worldwide turmoil strengthen my compassion and fuel my commitment to God's kingdom?

Notes based on the New Revised Standard Version by

George Wauchope

The Reverend Canon George Wauchope is tutor in World Mission Education at the Queens Foundation, Birmingham. He was an anti-apartheid activist in South Africa, was detained a number of times by the regime there and fled the country for Zimbabwe in 1989. He was ordained priest in 1996, was Dean of Studies at Bishop Gaul College in Harare and later became a parish priest in Botswana in 2002 before coming to the UK in January 2007.

In Africa, when a head of state visits another country, an advance party is sent to that country for security reasons. The party checks to ensure that the suite in which the head of state will sleep is not bugged, that there are no explosives there; and they also book themselves into strategic rooms next to the head of state in order to ensure his protection. They go to the places he is going to visit to make sure all is well. The advanced party is trained in what is called 'VIP protection'. A lot of money is spent on this, money that could otherwise be spent on alleviating the problems of the poor. And, incidentally, the security budgets for the countries that embark on this expensive exercise are usually three times the budget for health and education in those countries.

Well, the forerunner of the Prince of Peace is a 'maverick' called John the Baptist whose security concerns are the cleansing of the sinners through a baptism of repentance. For Jesus there is no VIP treatment. There is no room for him in the inn; he is born in a humble stable and is meek and mild. Does he need tight security? No! In fact he has come to lay down his life for the salvation and redemption of humankind. Compared to the heads of states referred to above, Christ is the Prince of Peace and of his reign there shall be no end.

Lord, help us fix our earth-bound longings on peace and justice in this world.

No VIP treatment

Luke 3:1-14

Words for Lent

George Wauchope

Reading 2

Salvation for the whole person

Luke 3:15-22

Luke begins his account of the public life of Jesus with a long introduction to the political and the religious leaders holding power at the time. He says: 'In the fifteenth year of Tiberius Caesar's reign' (verse 1). This would already be enough to arrive at the date, but he goes on giving the names of other important people: the governors of Palestine and of neighbouring territories, the high priests Annas and Caiphas. These VIPs played prominent roles during state functions and sat in prominent places for all to see.

Why all this detail? Luke wants us to keep clearly in mind that he is not about to tell us a nice fable, a myth, a legend, fruit of the extravagant imagination of some dreamer. The events he is about to write about are concrete history. God has intervened in the history of humankind at a clearly identifiable time and in a very definite place. God has sent his son to bring salvation to all humankind.

But the salvation brought by Jesus Christ must reach out to the whole person, to include every moment of our lives. It is this society, this community, this family, this concrete person that must be transformed. Thus the only true religion is the one that changes this world, that produces new relations among people and yields fruits of peace, love, justice and sharing where now there is greed, corruption, selfishness, oppression and injustice. Whenever we think of the reign of God, we should associate it with love, joy, peace, justice, righteousness and mutual respect.

In whatever we do, Lord, help us remember the fruits of the Spirit – love, joy, peace and the rest.

Jesus' mission statement, his manifesto as it were, is found in this passage. He is anointed by the Holy Spirit and sent by God his Father to proclaim good news to the poor. The only news that can be 'good' to the poor is the eradication of their poverty and its causes. And poverty means the lack of basic needs such as food, clean running tap water, clothing, shelter, health care and education.

Good news to the poor

Luke 4:16–30

Why is it that Africa is poor and cannot look after its own? The answer is colonialism, with its evil corollaries of military conquest, racism, economic and political subjugation, exploitation of cheap labour and the transportation of raw materials. In his book, *How Europe Underdeveloped Africa*, Walter Rodney explains in detail how this was done.

What really surprises me is that African leaders who sacrificed their lives in order to liberate their countries are the ones who behave like the shepherds that Ezekiel alludes to who do not eat and clothe the sheep but grab the resources of the land for themselves (Ezekiel 34:2b-4). How can close to two thousand people die of cholera in Zimbabwe today, a disease that is easily preventable? How can the sewage pipes burst with no money to repair them? How can a sane leader boldly state that there is no cholera when the death rate is increasing by the day? The man who placed his life in danger by fighting for the liberation of Zimbabwe has successfully run down that same country so that it is now on the edge of complete chaos.

Lord, may your message of good news transform the whole world and bring joy to those who are the most damaged members of our society.

2 Forerunners and followers

Notes based on the New Revised Standard Version by **Barbara Calvert**

Preparing for the week

God's people have always been on the move. Moses and the children of Israel, Abraham and Sarah, Joseph, Ruth, Mary and Joseph – all people on the move. God sending the Son, Paul and the apostles, missionaries throughout the ages, the Methodist movement – all are part of the ongoing, living story of God's people. What an awesome thought!

In recent years the exciting rediscovery of the God of the scriptures as a God of mission (*Missio Dei*, the mission of God) has inspired a shift from church understood as an institution to church as a movement. The church moving outside its comfort zones has led to a flowering of fresh expressions. A Fresh Expression is a form of church for our changing culture, established primarily for the benefit of people who are not members of any church (see www.freshexpressions.org.uk). In the first century there was no such thing as what we would recognise as traditional church. All was new; all was moving; and at the forefront were the forerunners and followers.

Barbara Calvert is a Methodist minister in the Orpington and Chislehurst circuit in Kent. Previously, she has been an RE teacher, worked for Christian Aid and ministered as a university chaplain in Glasgow.

For further thought

- What does it mean for you to be 'on the move'?
- How do you understand the *Missio Dei*?
- Who or what do you think of when you imagine 'forerunners and followers'?

In recent years, many churches have come to recognise that they are set in a time warp appealing only to those who are already members. Recognising that 'something needed to be done', some have thought that the solution lay in introducing guitars, new songs or changing the furniture by removing the pews. The expectation has been that if we just tweak things, make a few minor changes, then people will come in, new wine invited into roughly the same old wineskins.

In or out? Church walls

Luke 5:27–39

'He went out' (verse 27). A forerunner has to go out first. Jesus is out amongst the people demonstrating a radical newness about discipleship – and crowds of people are responding. Imagine a mission today. Levi responds to the call. What would our next move be? It could well be to invite him to church on Sunday morning!

But in this story Jesus' invitation to Levi is followed by Levi's invitation to Jesus to a banquet at his house. This exchange has established a relationship of mutuality and respect between the forerunner and the follower. Levi has not been humbled or humiliated. His dignity is intact, enabling him to grow and mature in faith, first as a follower and then further maturing into a forerunner himself. Jesus' willingness to go out brings about this transformation, and not only for Levi. Imagine the fun Jesus would have had at the banquet, the conversation and laughter. Life-changing encounters for all, through moving out!

What steps can I take to help my church become a church without walls?

Beckoning God, transform us by your grace.

Reading 5

Contemporary culture

Luke 6:12–26

Many churches today feel that they ought to tackle the widening gap that they have perceived between the majority of the population and the traditional church. They would like to become mission-shaped churches, sensing God's call to go out where people are. But they recognise that before they set out they must understand our present cultural setting, if the church is to be reshaped appropriately for its mission.

We might use terms such as 'consumerist', 'greed', 'cult of celebrities', 'big brother mentality' and 'populist' to describe our contemporary culture and think these are new phenomena. But Jesus warns his followers of just these very things! Beware, he says in the four woes, of having loads of money, being overfed, laughing at others and seeking to be popular and famous. Jesus knows that we need to understand contemporary culture in order to be shaped for mission, yet not be seduced by it. We are called to be in the world but not of the world.

The teaching of Jesus in these 'blessings' and 'woes' has hard lessons for all his followers. None of us feels up to the task any more than did the named and unnamed disciples, but we do have a choice. We can choose the way of the world or we can follow Jesus and take radical action to ensure a different future.

What steps can I take to help my church become culturally sensitive?

Reshaping God, transform us by your grace.

Barbara Calvert

My childhood holidays were always spent in Cornwall. For two weeks every August, my family stayed in a rented cottage in Trebetherick and every Sunday morning we went to Polzeath Methodist Church. I remember sitting in church with the sun pouring in, listening to the distant sound of the waves and children's voices from the beach. Yet it was peaceful inside, comfortable and welcoming – a traditional but happy experience of church even for a child. Now Polzeath is so popular with holidaymakers, surfers in particular, that local people can rarely afford to live there and just a few years ago Polzeath Methodist Church was facing closure.

However, the minister of the church had the vision to develop a Fresh Expression of church specifically for the surfing community. The church was pulled back from the brink of closure and is now enjoying a whole new lease of life as the Tubestation Church with skate ramp, plasma screens and café. Mostly young people are coming together, living out a 'Love thy neighbour' attitude both locally and globally and presenting the gospel in a way which is culturally relevant. The church now has forty regulars each week with several services on a Sunday, midweek Bible study classes and, during the summer months, struggles to fit everyone in.

'But is it church?' people ask. Jesus said, 'Look at the evidence'. 'Go and tell John what you have seen and heard' (verse 22).

What steps can I take to help my church become part of the Fresh Expression movement?

Exhilarating God, transform us by your grace.

Is it church?

Luke 7:18–35

Reading 7

Get into the boat

Luke 8: 22–25; 9:1–11

When I have been by the Sea of Galilee, I have imagined Jesus and the disciples walking by the shore. There is always a boat! In our story, Jesus invites his followers to go with him across to the other side of the lake. And even then they do not know exactly where they are going. They know it can be dangerous on the Sea of Galilee, but still they go. They could have said, 'No'. As often, out of nowhere, a storm blows up and it is frightening. The power of the wind and the waves is terrifying, but Jesus stills the storm and there is calm.

If these followers of Jesus had not had the courage to get into the boat, they would have missed the awesome experience of God's power in Jesus as he stills the storm. Only then are the disciples, empowered by what they have witnessed, ready and equipped to be sent out on a mission in God's name and with God's power.

Going out, being on the move, is risky and challenging but the disciples take the good news and cure diseases as they are instructed. They fulfil their mission, people's lives are changed and so too are the lives of Jesus' followers.

God's people today are being called to get into the boat. And just as the twelve go out as 'disciples' but return as 'apostles', so this is the possibility for the followers of Jesus today. It is indeed the only way.

What steps can I take to help my church become a church of apostles?

Empowering God, transform us by your grace.

Barbara Calvert

After much study, reflection, discussion and prayer, the people at one of the churches in Devon where I used to be minister decided to form a Fresh Expression of church. Conversations and enquiries had indicated that Saturday teatime would be a good time to start a group for young families, which we called 'The Ark'. This gave us the theme for the first gathering one Saturday in November 2007.

The story of Noah's Ark was told; children and adults then participated enthusiastically in all sorts of messy workshops related to the story. Then we all had a cooked tea together. After tea, the children enjoyed performing a dramatised, improvised version of Noah's Ark, and then we closed with singing and a time of reflection. It had been really hard work but families had come who were not members of the church, and one mother on leaving said, 'It was just like a party.'

It was just like a party: fun, participatory, noisy and boisterous – until the end. As the children took turns in lighting a candle and saying his or her own prayer, the sound of silence was powerful and the candlelight shone, if only momentarily. Our organising team went home exhausted but joyful. As followers of Jesus, we had accepted the gospel invitation to journey together up the mountain, and the experience had been transformational, for everyone.

What steps can I take to help my church become a transforming presence in society?

The transforming feast

Luke 9:18–36

Transforming God, transform us by your grace.

Reading 9

God goes ahead

Luke 10: 1–20

What is refreshing and exciting about the Fresh Expressions movement is the willingness of people to go out. A new energy, fired by God's Spirit, is setting men and women free of church structures, prepared to take risks, willing to learn from the world, recognising that God is already ahead of us in mission. In the early church too, they were not so arrogant as to think that the traffic was only one way. Jesus had taught them to recognise the signs of the kingdom in the world around them in unexpected people and places – in the Good Samaritan, the Syro Phoenician woman, the shepherd, the sower and the widow.

These seventy followers, men and women, are to accept hospitality given, offer a greeting of peace, and be sensitive to their hosts who might indeed already 'share in peace' (verse 6). They are instructed not to move from house to house. By staying in one house, rather than looking out for better lodgings, they have the opportunity to build kingdom relationships. Belonging before believing, putting human relationships at the heart of mission, allows the possibility for glimpses of God which might otherwise be missed.

Both forerunners and followers together are called to journey out, discovering and sharing in the transformational possibilities of being servants in someone else's house.

What steps can I take to help my church become a journeying people?

Journeying God, transform us by your grace.

Barbara Calvert

3 Making people whole

Notes based on the New Revised Standard Version by **Barbara Calvert**

Preparing for the week

We all long for healing. God too longs for our healing. Jesus was moved to compassion by suffering, and anxious to relieve the misery it entails. While there is much debate on how spiritual and medical healing relate to each other, I believe there is no distinction between the healing of medical science and divine healing. They are one, for this is God's world and nothing is outside God's domain. Our whole ministry is one of healing, and the ministry of healing is as much part of the Christian life as the ministry of preaching or service.

Every act of Christian worship celebrates the grace of God who desires the wholeness of body, mind and spirit for all people. In this sense, every service is a healing service and every aspect of worship – singing, praise, prayer, silence, confession – can contribute to the healing of both individuals and groups.

For further thought

- When and how have you experienced healing in your life?

- In what ways do you find worship, at its best, a healing experience?

- Think of individuals and communities in need of healing and pray for them.

Reading 10

Carer and cared for

Luke 7:1-17

The healing of the centurion's slave took place in Capernaum, and the healing of the widow's son in Nain. The precise geographical location of Nain is not known but Capernaum was a small fishing town on the shores of Lake Galilee. It was destroyed in the seventh century and now lies in ruins. I was in Capernaum a few months ago staring into the foundation stones of a home that evidence strongly suggests was Peter's house – the site of another healing story, the healing of his mother-in-law. Many can testify to a healing experience of some kind by simply being in such a place. This is because we are all in need of healing, of being made whole. This is the testimony of each of the readings this week.

Today's two stories also illustrate another fundamental truth: you cannot divide those in need of healing from those who care for them, for they too have a need of healing. It is the slave and the son who experience physical healing, but the centurion, who valued his slave highly, and the widow, who loved and depended on her son, also express their own need in asking for the healing of their dependent ones. Indeed, I myself have observed in my own experience that often the need of the carer is greater than the one being cared for.

Jesus restores to these two people the ones whom they loved, responding to their own need for wholeness too.

How do we recognise the healing that we need?

Caring God, heal us through your love.

Barbara Calvert

The other day, I visited an elderly member of our church who is now in a care home. In her time, she had been one of the church stalwarts. Always there when needed – at church teas, jumble sales, she helped in the Junior Church for years. She didn't like any fuss; she just got on with it: practical and dependable.

The one and the many

Luke 7:36-50

Now she is dependent on others. The care home is for those in the advanced stages of dementia. She didn't know me; she doesn't know anyone, neither family nor lifelong friends. She sits in her room all day, with the door open, making repetitive loud shrieks. Another resident stops and tells her that if she doesn't stop making that noise she will ring for her parents to take her home from school. It is surreal.

A young nurse slips into the room – gentle, kind and with a warm smile. She takes the old lady's hand and puts it against her face, gently caressing the woman's cheek with her own hand, drawing close. The old lady stops screeching; there is a response. The nurse tells me that gentle caressing, touch, is the only thing that the old lady responds to, but even this had taken time.

The nurse is infinitely patient; she pours out her love and care for this woman, as if she were the only one in the home that needed her. The lavishing of precious resources, our precious ointment, on the most vulnerable in our society is the pathway to wholeness for us all.

How do we learn how to pour out our whole self for the healing of God's world?

Vulnerable God, heal us through your love.

Words for Lent   Barbara Calvert

Reading 12

Naked and clothed

Luke 8:26-39

I am often invited to take assembly in the local primary schools. My usual approach is to tell a Bible story and the children act out the story as I tell it. A sea of eager hands goes up when I ask for volunteers to take part. Most of the children love to act, to dress up, to pretend to be someone else. The dressing-up clothes are very simple: just a black shawl for a widow, or a coloured shawl for a young woman, an Arabic scarf for Jesus or a disciple, simple hats for soldiers or guards. But these simple adornments transform the children and enable them to 'become' the character. What we wear expresses so much of who we are.

The demoniac wore no clothes at all, so who was he? He wasn't himself. Jesus asked him, 'What's your name?' and the man replied, 'Legion', because he was so many people all in one, so possessed by demons he didn't know who he was, with no clothes to identify him. We never discover the man's real name but we do know that, cured of his demon possession, he becomes a disciple in his home town, made whole by Jesus, his healing symbolised by being clothed.

How do we discover what are the new clothes of the kingdom?

Naked God, heal us through your love.

Barbara Calvert

Each member of our church is in a pastoral group with a specially designated person in the role of pastoral leader. Other roles held by people in the church include those of steward, property officer, worship leader and of course those who look after the money. We order our lives by dividing up our responsibilities. But, irrespective of roles, we may all pastor to one another at church and in our daily lives, simply by listening and caring. And every time we gather together in an act of Christian worship, we celebrate the grace of God who desires wholeness of body, mind and spirit for all people.

Jesus did not categorise people or his activities. His ministry of healing cannot be separated from his ministry of preaching and teaching; all of these are going on all the time to all people. The woman with the haemorrhage is physically healed but Jesus also listens to her story; in front of the whole crowd she told him everything. Imagine the effect on the crowd!

It is Jairus' daughter who is physically healed, but who else goes to bed that night changed? Not just her, but the girl's whole family, their friends and neighbours, members of the synagogue, Peter, John and James, the whole crowd – and, as we read and ponder, we too.

How do we use our own healing as a means of the healing of the whole of humanity?

Listening God, heal us through your love.

The individual and the crowd

Luke 8:40-56

Words for Lent

Barbara Calvert

Reading 14

Dogs and humans

Luke 9:37-50

Every Tuesday and Thursday afternoon a woman walked past the house where I used to live with her dog, Bonny. She was taking Bonny to the cottage hospital across the road to visit the patients suffering from mental illness, the elderly and frail and those recovering from strokes. The patients were greatly helped by Bonny's visits. Bonny was gentle, trusting, loyal and friendly, and a dog helped to keep them in touch with the world outside or brought back happy memories. On another occasion on holiday in France, I saw a man out with his dog. The man's face was terribly disfigured. But dogs do not see disfigurement or disability; they do not recoil from outward appearances. These dogs were contributing, perhaps unknowingly, to the healing and wholeness of human beings.

Our whole lives are a journey towards healing and wholeness. And some things will help that process and some things will hinder, as today's collection of stories illustrates. Distorted notions such as our own inferiority or greatness or that of others, of faith-healing over and above medical-healing, will hinder. Openness to God, a willingness to learn and journey in faith will help. All that contributes to healing of mind, body and spirit is of God.

How can we be more open to all the avenues of healing in our world?

Open God, heal us through your love.

Barbara Calvert

When I visit someone in hospital, it is often difficult to find them. Even if I know them well, patients lying in identical beds wearing nightclothes, without jewellery, make-up or usual hairdo can be very difficult to spot. Often they see me first – looking slightly lost. They smile, our eyes meet and contact is established. I then wonder how I could have failed to spot them immediately. My own problem in identifying someone in a hospital bed is illustrative of our tendency to compartmentalise people with an illness or disability: they become patients, or cancer sufferers or 'the disabled'.

To see or not to see

Luke 17:11-19

In today's story these ten people are identified by Luke by their illness – they are lepers. As lepers, they had to be treated differently, to be isolated. Thus they lost any individual identity of their own. We tend to assume they were all male, all Jewish – except one who was a Samaritan. But there could have been more who were Samaritans, and perhaps some of them were women. We know more about this one simply because he did not go with the crowd. He chose to set himself apart, to turn and recognise the source of his healing, to offer praise to God and be made whole, not simply cured of his leprosy.

How do we look beyond the labels to the common humanity that we all share?

Seeing God, heal us through your love.

Barbara Calvert

4   Living in the kingdom

Preparing for the week

Think of the kingdom (of God) as a way of living here and now rather than some non-identifiable world past or future. Think of a world that could be, here and now. Try not to think of what Jesus said as 'commandments – 'do this and the kingdom will come'. The kingdom cannot be achieved by our efforts. Think of it rather as something in the mind of God, which Jesus has a unique way of penetrating, and into which he shares his insights with us. Like a botanist walking through a very ordinary garden where most of us simply smile and nod, he stops us in our tracks with, 'Hey, look at this,' and then opens our eyes to what we are missing. The botanist helps us to see life in nature. Jesus helps us to see life in the kingdom. Call such a revelation a 'kingdom moment'. Jesus invites us to identify kingdom moments for ourselves. The kingdom is a given. Our privilege is to recognise it, practise its virtues, encourage its development and tell others.

Notes based on the Revised English Bible by **Alec Gilmore**

Alec Gilmore is a Baptist minister, Senior Research Fellow at the International Baptist Theological Seminary in Prague, and author of A *Concise Dictionary of Bible Origins and Interpretation* (Continuum).

For further thought

- Think of five situations where the Golden Rule ('Do to others what you would have them do to you', Matthew 7:12) is absolutely crucial and unquestionable. Think of another five where it could border on disaster.
- Make a list of your assets other than financial, evaluate your attachment to them and re-evaluate your priorities.
- When you next have a time of prayer with friends, spend at least 45 minutes sharing your kingdom moments before you pray.

The Golden Rule

Avoid Bibles with sectional headings as if to tell you what to find there. Practise reading the text for yourself. See it in relation to what went before and what happened next. Such interconnections often carry their own message. These verses, for example, raise tough questions about the ways we treat one another which go far beyond those we normally think of as 'enemies' and suggest how different life would be by a simple observance of the Golden Rule. Allowing truth to strike us in different ways can teach us a lot not only about the world but also about ourselves.

Luke 6:27-38

Recall an occasion when somebody got the better of you, damaged your reputation, hurt you or someone you love. What was your first reaction? To strike back? To call for justice? To seek compensation? All fairly natural and (depending on the circumstances) not necessarily unreasonable. Then think of someone you know, personally or from film, theatre or fiction, whose attitude instinctively would have been softer and shown more understanding. Which in the long run is likely to be more beneficial to the offender, to society and to your health? To find the answer is to glimpse the kingdom. To practise it is to participate in the kingdom.

Thank you, Father, for opening my eyes to a new world and a totally different way of living. Keep me always mindful of how I treat others and especially those who have offended me.

Reading 17

Catching the mirror

Luke 6:39-49

A strange collection of aphorisms here which don't immediately connect too readily with one another. Begin with questions. What might have led Jesus to make that remark about the blind leading the blind or the disciple who rated himself about his teacher? Did he have somebody in mind? And whatever caused his outburst in verse 42? Try recalling something in your own experience which might have led to any one of them.

Notice then the change of tone. The first two sayings (verses 39-40) are fairly objective. You know people like that. The third (verse 41) is different. It is addressed directly to me. I know because when I hear it I begin to feel uncomfortable. By verse 43 the window where I am looking out has become a mirror. I see myself. But which tree am I?

I pause. The mirror penetrates. This is not the doctor assessing a few external symptoms. This is an internal examination. It is a challenge to get a better understanding of myself and my relationship with others. Everything I say and do reflects what is inside. I see what he is driving at. Good people are not good because they do good things. They do good things because they are good people – inherently at peace with themselves and with God.

Kingdom bells are ringing – too loud for comfort. I turn the volume down and go away. 'Fine,' says Jesus, 'but don't forget the man who built a house without adequate foundations.'

Dear Lord, now I understand.

When the disciples asked to be taught to pray, what do you think they were asking for or expecting? If you asked your minister the same question, what would you be expecting? If a member of the congregation asked you, what might they be looking for? Learning words, phrases, sentences, liturgy maybe? A list of set times, how to stand, kneel, sit or hold your hands? Places to visit, perhaps. All may be helpful, some more than others, depending on the person asking the question, but they are not what Jesus goes for.

Learning to pray

Luke 11:1-13

Luke's shortened version of the Lord's Prayer and the accompanying story get down to basics. Prayer begins with attitude and relationship – first, with God (a recognition of who God is and how you see God); second, with life (food is vital for living and basic food for healthy living, as also is living a day at a time); third, with our fellow human beings (relationships and a proper sense of forgiveness for our failures which matures as we experience what our forgiveness of others means to others).

Simple basics maybe, but already we begin to wilt at the thought. More like weariness and hard work than immediate excitement which leads to exhilaration. Much easier to close our eyes and say the words. But that's what Jesus says it is, and the story seems to underline the point.

Dear Jesus, teach me first to think what to ask for, then give me the persistence to work at it.

Reading 19

Signs and blindness

Luke 11:29-36

Begin with the request for a sign. What did they want and what would have satisfied them? What sign could anyone have given that would not leave further space for doubt, question and argument? Better to ask a different question. Why were they asking? Recall any moment when you have caught yourself asking for 'proof' when the most you could only ever hope for was 'evidence' and how convincing would even that be, especially if you didn't want to believe it?

Underlying this question is a demand for certainty about something where certainty is not really possible. Precisely what led the Queen of the South to come from the ends of the earth to sit at the feet of Solomon nobody knows, but certainly something did, even if it was only her surmise that he had something of value to offer. Nor do we know what led the people of Nineveh to repent, save for the sharp realisation that what Jonah was going on about had about it the ring of truth. In both cases something grabbed them, and once hooked like that they really had no need or desire to go hunting for signs.

Jesus sees himself as holding up a lamp (just like any preacher). See it and your whole life may be transformed. Asking for signs may be an indication that you don't, in which case any number of 'signs' will make no difference. Kingdom moments don't come to order.

Lord, help me to see, especially when I find seeing difficult.

Alec Gilmore

Two key words here are 'anticipation' and 'expectation'. We are never going to see the kingdom if all we are engaged in is question, argument and discussion. Of course there are always going to be doubts and differences of opinion among believers (in all faiths) and exploration, discussion and even confrontation at times are appropriate responses. Sometimes they produce a kingdom moment of their own, provided we are not so engrossed in the argument that we fail to spot them.

Light your lamp, read the signs, be ready

Luke 12:35-53

Some of the best kingdom moments, however, are a by-product of people faithfully knowing what they are about and getting on with it, always prepared to admit that they may be wrong, and therefore prepared to change and adjust according to needs and circumstances, but always (and especially) alert to that moment when the light flashes, the drums roll and you suddenly become alive in a new way. It can happen any time and anywhere and if Peter wanted to lay claim to the experience for the elite he was doomed to disappointment – it can happen to anybody, and does.

It is a hard saying and a tough gospel. It makes sharp divisions between those who see and those who don't, and has been known to split families down the middle; but it is a sad day if we can read the runes of the weather, the environment and the economy and be blind to the kingdom moment.

Please God, keep me ever humble, ever faithful, ever watchful.

Words for Lent

Alec Gilmore

Reading 21

Lose your assets

Luke 18:18-30

This is more than a hard saying about the penalties of wealth. Riches are not the only asset. Look more closely.

This man is 'a ruler'. He knows something about power and control. He needs to know where he is, and where other people are. His strength comes from his position (as a ruler) and from the fact that he has kept the rules – always. So why is he worrying about eternal life? Either his life is not fully satisfying or he wants Jesus to be more specific. Jesus plays along with him and the ruler knows the stock answers. So Jesus tries another line. Literally, it is a statement about wealth, but Jesus might have meant at least two other things.

One, forget your assets and embrace a totally different way of life. Sell up. Take off. Start again somewhere else. A challenge to people who have nothing as it is to those who have much, as the disciples knew only too well. Peter says as much. 'We have – so what?'

Two, consider whether you are looking in the wrong place for what it is you are hoping to find. Don't look for fresh fish in the depths of the ocean or tigers in Africa – they are not there. What you are looking for may not sit comfortably with what you treasure. Jesus had hit the nail on the head and the ruler knew it.

Father, it is time for a stocktaking, and please help me to surrender without waiting to discover the rewards.

5 Stories of the kingdom

Notes based on the Revised English Bible by **Alec Gilmore**

Preparing for the week

Having opened our eyes to kingdom moments, Jesus proceeds to tell stories of kingdom values. Stories about what it is like living in the kingdom; about the qualities which need to be cherished, similar to those later noted by Paul as the fruits of the spirit (Galatians 5:22-23).

Kingdom values are universal and honoured in different ways and to varying degrees in most if not all religions. Most of them need little defence, though the devil as always is in the detail and there is room for wide diversity in application. If kingdom moments identify the kingdom, kingdom values tell us where to spot it. As with moments, their very nature takes us by surprise and there may well be some slight twist which pulls us up with a jerk, making us think again and possibly leading to adjustments in our attitudes or lifestyle.

Some stories also have more than one kingdom value. Just because you are familiar with a story, don't imagine you know everything it is saying before you begin. Try writing down what you feel the kingdom value is before you read the notes. The notes try to focus on one. See if it is the same. Perhaps you can spot others.

For further thought

- What values are reflected in the story of the Good Samaritan? How many are genuine kingdom values?

- Consider the price paid by those around you to enable you to believe and do the things that you are committed to.

Reading 22

Knowing myself

Luke 8:1-18

Taken out of context, verses 5-8 lend themselves to allegorical interpretation and most preachers have taken advantage of this, identifying the crowd variously according to their readiness to believe. In context it may have a wider interpretation. This tour (verse 1) is not an evangelical campaign or a comfort zone for believers, and the parable may be taken as a comment on life. It is how people are – how we all are.

Imagine a stranger with an odd collection of followers suddenly arriving in your town. The locals all react in very different ways, and it's the same everywhere. His entourage can't understand it and he knows it. He, on the other hand, sees very clearly what is happening and shares it with them, possibly to enlighten, possibly to see how perceptive they are. Apparently they aren't, so he has to spell it out for them.

Try reading it not as a story about believers and unbelievers but about all of us. And not only about faith but about everything we touch. Some see, some don't. Some start, some finish. Some cop out, some struggle to stay in. It doesn't have to be a judgemental parable, though it does suggest that those who hear and persist are likely to make the most of their lives and this does represent a challenge to his immediate hearers (the disciples) to sort themselves out.

Thank you, Jesus, for opening my eyes to see myself and others in a different way.

Alec Gilmore

Words for Lent

28

Instead of beginning with the lawyer, begin with the disciples returning from a preaching mission (verse 17), overwhelmed by their success, not by numbers but by the sort of people they have picked up. Not 'the learned and the wise' but the 'simple' – people whose capacity for seeing and hearing outshines that of the clever and the bright. The lawyer just doesn't get it, and if he does he is not happy about it. It doesn't fit in with his expectations. How does it relate to eternal life? Living and working on a different planet, he listens on a different wavelength. And there are 'lawyers' in all professions and none, with similar emotions and queries. Think of some.

Basic humanity

Luke 10:25-37

Next, instead of spotlighting the Samaritan, with the familiar dig at the faithful and the statutory medal for the outsider, the rejected and the marginalised, reflect on other basic human attitudes in the story. In a tight spot, where do you find kingdom values and where are they missing? Ask people who collect for charity where it is easiest and hardest to knock on doors and with what result. Identify stories of people who willingly share resources and people who find good reasons for not. Ask yourself questions about the exclusive defensiveness and self-protection of religious people when it comes to faith and customs. Preserving purity usually gets more votes than costly redemption.

Dear Jesus, never let my determination to protect what I have prevent me hearing the cry from those in need.

Reading 24

Justice and fairness

Luke 12:13-34

Possessions need not be a problem. The desire to hang on to them, to control them and to use them to control others is. The kingdom is not about claiming divine authority for what we want. Jesus refuses to get involved and turns our attention to the underlying sense of greed and power. Forget the negatives here (verses 22ff). We need food, we need clothes, and you can't start afresh with everything every morning. There are other issues and going down that road may be a useful way of avoiding them.

Think of tensions, which may be inevitable and necessary and can also be creative, rather than black and white, right and wrong. Many tensions lurk here. Tension between possessions themselves and our attachment to them is only one. There is the tension between having enough to live reasonably and an over-reaching grasping mentality; between what we would like and what we really need; between reasonable concern and unreasonable anxiety (verse 29). You can no doubt think of others.

Justice is both a kingdom value and a human right, and at all levels includes basic fairness, sensible rationality and human understanding. Commitment to kingdom values is not the same thing as getting what you want or advancing your cause. It is more about recognising and appreciating those fundamental qualities of life that never wear out, last for ever and (as values) can never be taken away.

Thank you, Jesus. Your stories so help me to keep kingdom-centred.

Alec Gilmore

Words for Lent

Ho! Ho! (verse 15). If the kingdom is so great let's make sure we get a front seat. 'Oh dear,' says Jesus, 'they still don't get it.' Another story needed.

These people don't know a bargain when they see one. It's a generous invitation. A free gift. Well worth having. Great on a Sunday when it comes. Who could not respond? Nothing changes and there's nothing wrong with it by the time they get to Wednesday or Thursday – just that it gets low priority when the time comes and it has to compete with everything else that has to be done. A side effect is that kingdom values then turn up somewhere else as the householder's overwhelming generosity breaks through. He turns his attention elsewhere. First the second eleven, then all the people he had never even thought of befriending or co-operating with. Those on the far horizon are suddenly centre stage with an opportunity to enjoy something they never thought would come their way, and the absentees are left to work it out for themselves without a word of encouragement.

But then there is no such thing as a free lunch. A price has to be paid (verses 25-27), and often not only by those who enjoy the feast. So we must think before we jump. Pause to count the cost, to ourselves but also to others.

Father, keep me ever mindful of the people who pay a price for my commitment. May I never take it for granted.

Reading 26

Crisis time

Luke 16:1-17

References to dishonesty and an 'unjust steward' can be misleading. As in a stop-and-search operation this man is under suspicion (verse 1) and feels the dice of justice loaded against him. He knows and fears the worst, and in a tight spot turns to his friends. They may not save him but he will need them when he comes out. You may be able to identify him, not very far away.

Begin with his emotions. What if he knew he had done wrong and had been rumbled? What if he knew he hadn't but feared he was being victimised? And what about his master? Is he honourable, is he being got at, is he genuinely seeking truth or has he already made his mind up?

Avoid the issues of right or wrong. There is not enough evidence to make a judgement and Jesus doesn't go down that road either. The Greek translated as 'dishonest' (verse 8) can simply mean 'to do wrong'. Similarly avoid the argument as to whether the master is the householder or Jesus. Both may well have agreed that his handling of the crisis was 'wrong' but the master applauds him 'for acting so astutely' (verse 8), and in the second half of the verse Jesus seems to wish that all God's people were a bit more like him.

Please God, help me not to rush to judgements on others until I have entered into their emotions, established the facts and worked out what I might have done in their shoes.

Alec Gilmore

Words for Lent

In Brecht's *Galileo* there is a reference to the need to look not to the ceiling but the sky. In Tennessee Williams's *Stairs to the Roof*, we have an office clerk working in a sweatshop on the top floor of a 12-storey building. He doesn't fit the system, rebels against the rigidity and tells his boss he wants to go higher. His matter-of-fact boss explains that since they are already on the top floor there is nowhere higher to go. 'But there is,' says the man, 'there are stairs to the roof.' Nobody had ever found them, but he often retreated to enjoy the sky. His boss was content with the ceiling. Kingdom people are sky-people.

Ceiling-people know what they want, are single-minded and preoccupied with the satisfaction that comes from the fulfilment of their dream. Dives is a 'ceiling' character. He was not unaware of Lazarus. He instantly recognised him and knew his name (verse 23) but Lazarus was not part of his world until Dives was in dire straits and even then he only wanted him as his lackey. Dives lives in a closed world, his mind closed to God and his heart to compassion. He is sensitive to his brothers to a point (verse 28) but still fails to appreciate that they were well aware of the teaching and if they were not convinced on moral grounds they were highly unlikely to be changed by Lazarus.

Thank you, Father, for the warning. Keep me always reaching for the sky.

The ceiling and the sky

Luke 16:19-31

6 Confrontation in Jerusalem

Preparing for the week

The ministry of Jesus is, in so many ways, a story of journeying. Because we know the beginning and ending of the story, we expect the events that unfold. It's inevitable that Jesus will die, inevitable (at least to us) that he will rise again at the end of the story. Part of the difficulty with the end of the story is that its familiarity leads us into complacency. Luke, who wrote his gospel towards the end of the first century AD for a predominantly gentile community, was keen to stress the universal nature of God's salvation through Jesus. Central to this was the death, resurrection and ascension of Jesus. It was these dramatic events that brought a new hope to all, but especially to those whom society marginalised. This brought about a new community expressed through the idea of the kingdom of God, an idea which brought with it outreach, but also embrace to all people. The 'good news' meant a reversal of fortune for many, and it is helpful not to forget the radical nature of this gospel message, nor the implications for our contemporary faith. The events of Passion Week, as presented by Luke, are perhaps best described as a journey to transformation, a journey in which all participate as children of God.

Notes based on the *New Testament Study Guides* 'freshly translated' by Nicholas King (Kevin Mayhew 2004) by **Helen-Ann Hartley**

Revd Dr Helen-Ann Hartley is Tutor in New Testament at Ripon College, Cuddesdon, and curate in the parish of Littlemore, Oxford. In addition to her college and parish duties, she is a frequent broadcaster for BBC Oxford and BBC Ulster.

For further thought

- In what ways do you see yourself and your community needing transformation?
- What is your prayer as you begin the journey of Holy Week – for yourself and for others?

All four gospel writers record the events of Jesus' arrival into Jerusalem, but Luke has some distinctive features. One of the most interesting is that the joyful reception of Jesus takes place on the top of the Mount of Olives itself, just as Jerusalem is coming into view. If there's one thing that is certain about Jesus' ministry, it's that there was always something different around the corner, or as in the case of today's passage, up a mountain. In the Bible, mountains are frequently places of revelation, and this passage is, in many ways, about finding out more of who Jesus is. Mountains too can represent a shift in perspective; things look different from the top, and perhaps we feel different too once we are 'up there'.

An unexpected entry

Luke 19:29-40

People cope in various ways when bad things happen, but one thing that most people need to do is to be able to tell their story. That might take some time, but it is often in the action of speaking out loud that we come to terms with what has happened to us. That is the point at which transformation may take place. Christians believe that the ultimate transformation takes place beyond this life, and this is the story of Easter itself. In Western culture, which doesn't 'do' mystery and wonder very well at all, all this business of resurrection seems completely unbelievable. But that's the whole point of Passion Week. The drama is unexpectedly shocking, and Luke begins as he ends – with an unexpected turn of events.

God of our journeying, help us to prepare to welcome Christ as we travel with him through the events of this week. May we meet him in the places and people that we encounter.

Words for Lent

Helen-Ann Hartley

Reading 29

And they rejoiced?

Luke 19:41-48; 22:1-6

Jesus weeps over Jerusalem, whilst others looking to capture him rejoice. The scene is set for the events that rapidly begin to unfold. The description of Jesus weeping over Jerusalem has been influenced by the laments of Hebrew prophets, as well as the descriptions of the destruction of the Temple by the Jewish historian Josephus and others. Whereas Luke elsewhere expands on Mark's version of events, when it comes to the driving out of the sellers in the Temple, Luke's account is terse. For Luke, the Temple's importance lay much further back in the story, when the elderly Simeon proclaimed Jesus' birth from within the Temple. Now Luke wants to move events on beyond the bounds of the Temple.

The second part of our passage moves the story on further, with the shocking news that it is from amongst Jesus' closest associates that betrayal is located. People in power struggles often need a 'mole' on the other side, and in Judas they find one. Judas agrees to the plan which, in the Greek, is the language of confessing. The irony runs deep: rejoicing and confessing. The reality of the situation couldn't be further from that truth.

What difference can your faith make to the situations of power struggle that you encounter?

God of weeping and rejoicing, you share in our trials and sorrows. Be with us always, that we may know the light and peace of your presence when we feel most alone.

Helen-Ann Hartley

The apparent ordinariness of sharing the Passover is both transformed and shattered by Jesus' actions. Jesus has clearly looked forward to sharing this meal with the disciples before he must 'suffer'. There is a close similarity in the words for 'Passover' and 'suffer' (in the Greek, *pascha*), and we are surely meant to pick up on the word-play. For Luke, Jesus' story is one that we all share in, and this part of the narrative emphasises the importance of participation. Luke is not so focused on the complexities of what Jesus' death meant in itself. Rather, through the very act of sharing in the meal, we are all participants in God's kingdom, that's the point of it all.

Meal times can be points of celebration, sharing in news, coming together as a family at the end of a busy day. But meal times nowadays are most often disparate and hurried affairs. Too many other things compete for our attention, we just don't have time to sit and eat together. The disciples receive the dreadful news that a betrayer is in their midst. What follows is predictable: an argument. 'It's not me!' You can almost hear the conversation. The story of Judas teaches us not to be naïve, either about ourselves or about those around us who call themselves Christians.

Have you ever been betrayed by someone? What did that feel like?

God who suffered, forgive us when we deny that we know you or when we reject your presence amongst us. Help us to be mindful of the needs of others, and never to be so complacent that we stand by when others are scorned in your name.

A meal and an argument

Luke 22:7-23

Reading 31

Jesus? Never heard of him

Luke 22:24-38

Luke continues his gospel theme of the reversal of fortunes with the first part of our passage for today. The houses in which Christians met for worship were designed architecturally to reinforce the social status of the owner, who would recline comfortably and be served by slaves. The idea of the greatest becoming like the servant would have been incredibly offensive and shocking.

Another shocking turn of events follows, with the news of Peter's denial. The structure of Jesus' words both emphasises Jesus' own prayer for Peter, and Peter's faith. At this point, the contrast between Matthew's and Luke's narratives is interesting: after Peter denied Jesus, Matthew never mentions his name again, but Luke goes on to recount Peter's speech at Pentecost. Peter is every inch the example of someone who is redeemed after a terrible act of rejection.

The final part of the passage picks up on the instructions about travelling that Luke has already mentioned much earlier (in chapter 10). But the picture has apparently changed somewhat, and the previous instructions are to be ignored. The reference to the 'two swords' seems odd, but what seems to be presented is a classic Lukan image of fulfilment. Here the reference is to the 'Suffering Servant' passages in Isaiah 53. Perhaps Jesus' farewell discourse is pointing to a future tension between Jesus' successors and society?

When do we deny Jesus?

Hear us, Lord, as we turn to the events of your death. As the mood turns to darkness, may we catch glimmers of hope and light.

Helen-Ann Hartley

In this passage Luke concentrates on Jesus' prayer rather than the failure of the disciples to support Jesus in his hour of need. The fact that Jesus twice tells his disciples to pray is significant. Jesus' struggle is then supported by the presence of an angel. Although we should note that verses 43 and 44 appear to be a later textual interpolation, there is good reason for Luke to have included these verses as a proper understanding of the struggle that Jesus endured at this point, rather than understanding it simply as an experience of 'agony'. Interestingly too, Luke omits the name of the place in which Jesus prayed. There is no mention of 'Gethsemane'. The use of the language for 'sleeping' is best understood as metaphorical language which Luke uses to emphasise the cosmic nature of the unfolding drama. This is not just a human story, but it is God's story too.

Why me? Why now?

Luke 22:39-53

Notice how Jesus takes steps to prepare the disciples for the future; it is Jesus who takes the initiative in addressing Judas. Furthermore, even in this most desperate of times, Jesus continues his ministry of healing. There is much irony in Jesus' words when he questions those who try to arrest him as a robber. Significantly, Jesus seems to be in control of events at this point. Everything he has done has led up to this point, and the prophetic words of Isaiah, that Jesus would be arrested with the lawless, are being fulfilled here in this passage.

Lord, we pray that during this time of struggle, we may find strength and compassion to accompany you as you accompany us throughout our lives.

Words for Lent

Helen-Ann Hartley

Reading 33

Bitter tears?

Luke 22:54-71

It is hard to imagine how Peter must have felt at this point. Given his earlier protestation that he would never deny knowledge of Jesus, for this to happen was devastating. Luke's remark that Jesus 'turned and looked' at Peter is a pivotal point in the story. Luke again highlights Jesus' prophetic presence as Peter remembers the word that the Lord had spoken. The reaction is a weeping of bitter tears.

Although in Luke's account the council meets formally in the morning when the examination of Jesus takes place, it has less characteristics of a trial than have Matthew and Mark's night session of the council: there are no witnesses, no formal accusation and no condemnation of Jesus. The council's focus is on the status of Jesus, and Jesus replies in a way that does not fall into their trap, but instead defines his status in terms which transcend their own categories. The term 'Son of God' is significant for Luke (more so than 'Christ'), because it harks back to the angel's declaration to Mary in 1:35, and anticipates the preaching in Acts 9:20 and 13:33. With a hint of irony, Luke has the members of the council declare that they have 'heard from his mouth'. The point that Luke wants us to get is that they haven't really 'heard' at all because if they had, then Jesus would not be in the position he is at this point in the narrative.

Loving God, as we weep bitter tears with Peter, we pray for those who are tempted to deny you through fear of persecution. May your presence strengthen them.

7 The way of the cross

Notes based on the
New Revised
Standard Version by
Godfrey Chigumira

Preparing for the week

It is natural that we tend to enjoy gospel commentaries that cheer us up and leave us feeling joyful. But the way of the cross, though good news, is no cheerful event. Neither is the overall condition of many Africans' lives. In writing these notes I have had to struggle between a desire to uplift my readers, on the one hand, and making an honest reading of Africans' lives from the passion narrative, on the other. My sense of honesty won the day, and I hope that what I have written will deepen readers' sense of the passion of Christ which continues in the world today. I speak not for all Africans, but out of my own particular context and experience.

For further thought

- Where do you see Christ continuing to walk the way of the cross in today's world?
- In what ways do you experience the struggle between honesty and the desire to find a word that uplifts?

Godfrey Chigumira grew up in Zimbabwe, southern Africa, and served as a priest there for five years before coming to the United Kingdom. He is currently working in Hawarden Benefice in North Wales, and researching the figure of Mary as a source of empowerment for women with HIV Aids.

Reading 34

A cry for justice for the poor and the weak

Luke 23:1-12

The two trials of Jesus in this passage portray a profound miscarriage of justice. Pilate finds Jesus innocent (verse 4), but will not execute justice by releasing him. Pilate is unable to stand for truth at the expense of his own reputation. He tries to avoid his responsibility of giving Jesus a fair trial by referring him to Herod (verse 7). On the other hand, Herod is only interested in being entertained by Jesus (verse 8). The chief priests make inaccurate and false accusations about Jesus, and get what they want from Pilate by threatening his position with Caesar (verse 2). The trials lack honesty and compromise justice.

The human rights records of the justice systems in Africa are often very poor. In different African countries, there is a backlog of untried cases, with the accused often locked up in detention without trial for many months. This is especially true of some political prisoners and of those who are too poor to afford legal representation. When the trials happen, justice and fairness do not always prevail. Political motivations and propaganda often outweigh a right concern for justice. At the same time, the rich and those who hold political power may get away with committing terrible crimes without being brought to trial. The justice systems themselves are often deliberately built to favour those in political power.

What does it take to transform unjust systems into ones that are just?

Lord, stand alongside those who are unjustly tried, and bring to justice those whose crimes cry out to heaven.

Godfrey Chigumira

In the last half of the twentieth century, the word 'independence' sounded like sweet music in the ears of many Africans. After many a bloody struggle, many of them achieved freedom from colonial rule during that period. Wild celebrations ensued, and independence was understood to be pregnant with possibilities once only dreamt about. However, in more than a few cases, those dreams have now blown away and dissipated like the wind. With little or no marked difference in their plight, many Africans today still labour and toil for their day-to-day survival. 'Independence' has become little more than an empty word. After the colonialist came the dictator, the corrupt ruler, the violent leader, the self-centred president, economic mismanagement, and so on.

Jesus is tossed back and forth between Pilate and Herod. In the passion narrative, this could be his fifth or sixth trial within twelve hours. Like the other trials, this one is unjust, harrowing and full of violent images. Pilate is the foreign invader, the colonialist, and Herod the local oppressive ruler. For the ordinary Africans too, injustice, violence and corruption have remained part of life regardless of the particular ruler. They too are tossed back and forth from one oppressive system to another, and from one oppressor to the other. Their short lifespan of poverty, pain and lack of economic and political freedom continues.

Pray for those caught in the cycle of injustice, violence and corruption – and that God will raise up those who will bring real change to Africa.

The long walk to freedom

Luke 23:13-25

Words for Lent

Godfrey Chigumira

Reading 36

'Daughters of Africa, weep for yourselves!'

Luke 23:26-31

Jesus turns and speaks to the women, but not to Simon who is labouring under his cross. Is this an oversight on Jesus' part? Probably not, from one African context.

Many African women love being mothers and having children. They work very hard to bring up their children and to care for the daily needs of their male partners. Concern for their own lives usually comes last. At the same time many women depend heavily on their male partners for the resources needed to run the family. However, the men do not always provide enough for the family upkeep. Many African men, like Simon, carry heavy crosses in the form of little reward for heavy industrial and manual labour, hard and long labour shifts. Many African men struggle to find any employment. This makes it difficult for women to care for the family, and they are the ones who usually feel the full weight of their men's crosses. Under their often limiting husbands' authority, many women also lack the power to change such bad situations, and the realisation of their full potential is often thwarted and suffocated.

Lord, to the daughters of Africa, you say the same: 'Cry for yourselves.' Encourage and empower these daughters to seek self-empowerment, so that, like the central pillar in a house, they can support and improve not only their lives, but those of their children and their male partners as well.

Godfrey Chigumira

How about this for a fable? 'Once upon a time the creator visited his creatures, and the creatures said him, "You are so evil you deserve to die". So the creatures got hold of their creator and killed him.' It sounds like a story of satirical irony!

However, if taken more seriously, as an event that actually happened, significant and hard lessons can be drawn from this fable. Humans have badly erred and, without proper care, they continue to do so. They need to be more careful, especially where others' lives are concerned.

In the killing of Jesus, the mistake of pronouncing a death sentence on one who does not deserve it comes into today's spotlight. Still widely practised by most African countries, the ultimate penalty is fraught with many dangers. It presupposes our surefootedness in judging others, and it betrays our failure to realise how ill-equipped and defective our judgements can often be. It takes humility to acknowledge that we are not good enough to give others the ultimate penalty. The death-sentence mentality can also encourage violence on offenders by the offended in society. One violent act begets another, leading to a cycle of violence. Rather than a sign of respect for life, the death sentence itself can be a symptom of a widespread lack of sanctity of life.

May no created person find another unworthy of life.

The death sentence

Luke 23:32-43

Reading 38

A watching that transforms

Luke 23:44-49

They 'stood at a distance, watching these things' (verse 49). They watched the things that transpired at Jesus' expiration. These were not pleasant things to watch: darkness, the sun's light failing, Jesus calling out his last words loudly and in pain and breathing his last. As they watched, they must have tried to decipher the meaning of what was happening. Their knowledge of him, of how he had bettered almost every situation, would have encouraged them to think about the meaning of this, and would have given them hope for a better outcome.

The death of infants due to curable disease, the preventable deaths of young parents and of people due to poverty, AIDS, tuberculosis, malaria and state-sponsored violence, the lack of medicine and medical expertise – there is so much to watch in Africa today, and what a painful experience it is to see it. Yet watching by itself does not change anything! It is when that experience is brought before Jesus' cross from which the resurrection is born that it can bear fruit. From Jesus' cross lessons can be learnt and new insights borne into our own experiences. The curtain of the old order of things can be torn in two (verse 45) to give way to the new era where these evils become things of the past.

Dear Lord, turn the darkness of our continent into the light of your resurrection.

Godfrey Chigumira

Have you ever seen a dog sitting before the grave of its master after the master's burial? Or do you remember your feelings during and soon after the burial of someone really close to you? One can experience a strange, sour feeling of weakness, vulnerability and even shallowness. One can feel as if in an unfamiliar and threatening territory. It can be difficult to resume normal life again.

Bereavement in Africa

Luke 23:50-56

Many African societies have large families, but also a short lifespan and many premature deaths. Africa is rampant with multiple untimely bereavements and long periods of mourning. It is a terrible time for those who must endure the loss of those they love. Africans' experiences of emptiness and loneliness come into my mind when I read about Jesus' burial and the women who followed from Galilee. With one's feelings in turmoil, it is not easy to find rest (verse 56) in heart and soul after such loss. It is most likely that the day of rest was for these women a time when their feelings of loss fully confronted them. However, the gaping hole left by Jesus' death and burial was soon filled, for the original women, by his resurrection. For many Africans today, that gap often remains a prolonged austere experience that fails to heal.

Lord Jesus, may your short lifespan induce in us the will and energy to improve the lives of young parents and children who die early in life.

The risen Lord

Notes based on the New Revised Standard Version by
Paul Nicholson SJ

Easter Day

The women at the beginning of this passage know exactly where they are going, and what they have to do. They have a duty to honour the dead Jesus by tending to his corpse. Even without this duty, their love for him would have led them to this task. It remains, though, a desperately sad job to have to carry out, and furthermore one without hope.

Paul Nicholson is a Roman Catholic priest belonging to the Society of Jesus (the Jesuits). He is currently Director of Novices in Britain, and has worked since ordination in the fields of spirituality and social justice.

The message of the two men they meet in the tomb changes all of that. Although the women are terrified by the men's appearance, the news that Christ is risen still gets through to them, and serves to remind them of all that Jesus has said. So there is no longer any need to stay among the graves and corpses. Filled now with hope, they set out again, this time as witnesses of what Christ means in their own lives.

Is there anything in your own experience that echoes the change in these women? Can you remember times when dutiful service kept you shackled to ways of living and patterns of behaviour which were anything but life-filled? Or when a new way of looking at things led you on into a greater freedom? Maybe that is a gift you might want to ask for today, for yourself or someone close to you.

Why look for the living among the dead?

Luke 24:1–12

For further thought

- How does the light of the resurrection illuminate your own life?
- How can you share something of that illumination with others?

International Bible Reading Association

How to order

If you found help and inspiration from using *Words for Lent,* you may well enjoy *Words for Today*, our annual book of Bible reading notes from which the readings in this sampler come. A full list of the readings can be found on our website:

www.christianeducation.org.uk/ibra

- online at http://shop.christianeducation.org.uk/
- by emailing sales@christianeducation.org.uk
- by phone 0121 472 4242
- by post, returning the form overleaf to:
  IBRA
  1020 Bristol Road
  Birmingham
  B29 6LB

Words for Today is published annually in August for the following calendar year.

Please contact IBRA for up-to-date prices.

The books are also available on cassette each month through Galloways Trust for the Blind. Please contact IBRA direct for more details.

Order form

Please contact IBRA for up-to-date prices.

Name: _____

Address: _____

_____

_____

_____ Postcode: _____

Telephone number: _____

Code		Quantity	Price	Total
	IBRA List of readings*		FREE	FREE
	Words for Today			
	P&P is free in the UK			
	Total			

* Free with any purchase; unlimited copies within reason

☐ I would like the latest Christian Education catalogue sent free

☐ I enclose a cheque (made payable to IBRA)

☐ Please charge my MASTERCARD/VISA/SWITCH

Card Number: ☐☐☐☐☐☐☐☐☐☐☐☐☐☐☐☐ Issue Number: ☐☐

Expiry Date: ☐☐ ☐☐

Security number (last three digits on back): ☐☐☐

Signature: _____

Please return this form to
IBRA
1020 Bristol Road
Selly Oak
Birmingham
B29 6LB

The International Bible Reading Association is a Registered Charity